My Heart's Therapy

Brenda Kishiyama

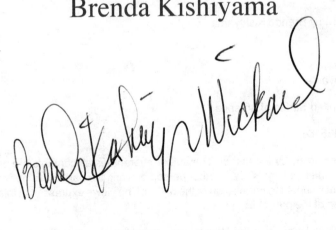

My Heart's Therapy
by Brenda Kishiyama

Printed in the United States of America.

ISBN 9781498465168

www.xulonpress.com

Dedication

To my oldest–my inspiration

To my youngest–my reminder that God's timing is perfect

Acknowledgements

To my God, the giver of all things
To all my divine appointments, including family and friends –
you know who you are

Table of Contents

Anxiety and Loneliness: 13

My Rock 14
The Voice 17
Focus On Him 20
Remember Me 23
Here I Am 26
He Created Me 29

Failure: 32

Saved Again 33
Every Day 36
Temptation 39
Go His Way 42
If I Choose Him 45

Strength In Weakness: 48

Lord Teach Me To Pray 49
Let Us Go 52
Godly Woman 55
I Am The One 58
I Will Be There 61

<u>Contentment Through Adversity</u>: 64

This Race Called Life 65
Just Give Me Jesus 68
Dear Father 71
Knockin On My Door 74
180 Degrees 77
Forever Love 80

<u>Joy – No Matter What</u>: 83

Let Your Light Shine 84
Give It All To Me 87
Singing His Praises 90
My Jesus 93
I Want To Thank You 96
Calling Your Name 99

Preface

My Heart's Therapy was created during a time when I found myself wanting to run away. I was discontent, yet knew I was in that place for a reason. So, I began to search for answers that could release me from my discontentment. One night, as I was rocking my son to sleep, my feelings released as a tune in my head. Out of curiosity, I wrote the lyrics down. Over the next two months I continued to write down a flood of my thoughts and feelings, which turned into lyrics to about two dozen songs. I was convinced those words were answers from God. I knew he had flooded my head with words and promises to assure me, strengthen me, console me, and push me forward. He had heard me cry out to Him. He knew I had been searching; I waited with a patience I didn't know I possessed, and listened for His guidance as to what direction I should go. What did he want me to do with this music from my heart?

In the meantime, I desperately sought out knowledge from the Bible and through Bible studies—excitedly pursuing a deeper relationship with God. As I quietly waited for His direction, it became clear that he was calling me, an unlikely writer, to spread His word through song. I had no choice but to write. Words flowed freely because they were not my thoughts—they were His. His word cannot be silenced. His voice; however, became silent in regards to the music and I pursued life, clinging tightly to Him. At the time, it was suggested I look at the words I had written down as healing for myself, to let it go, and to just move on. I felt in my heart God had more purpose for the music and for me, but I set it aside and let it go. One day, I felt God say, "Now! Now is the time." As I revisited those songs, years later, I realized it had been therapy—therapy for my heart and soul. It was time to share the therapy with others.

It is my prayer that God's glory will be achieved through these songs. And that you will identify with, find solace in, be encouraged by, and be motivated to search for your own answers in your relationship with Jesus Christ.

Love in Christ,
Brenda

> Wait for the Lord;
> Be strong and take heart
> And wait for the Lord.
> Psalm 27:14

Anxiety and Loneliness

<u>Relinquishment</u> – to let go; surrender.

Why is it I have to pry my clenched fists open finger by finger? Why do I hang on so hard when I could just open them up and <u>let go and let God</u>? Oh to be free of worry. What an amazing way to live. And we can. <u>He takes care of everything. We just have to let him work</u>. In my humanness, I struggle with this concept and yet I strive for it as well. I know my whole being would be so much healthier if I could just let go.

"Therefore I tell you, do not worry about your life, what you will eat or drink; or about your body, what you will wear. Is not life more important than food, and the body more important than clothes? Look at the birds of the air; they do not sow or reap or store away in barns, and yet your heavenly Father feeds them. Are you not much more valuable than they? Who of you by worrying can add a single hour to his life?"
Matthew 6: 25-27

My Rock

New town. New space. All around a new face.
New church. New friends. I feel lost once again.
Close my eyes and pretend I'm an eagle in the wind.
Fly away. Fly away. Another place. Another day.
But one thing remains the same.
One insult. Then another. Beat down yet again.
Accusations fly. Can't say why.
Another relationship gone awry.
Like a turtle in his shell try to run from private hell.
Feel like I'm going insane.
But one thing remains the same.
A family is a gift, but sometimes there are rifts.
If anger is your drug the pressure will build up.
Like a lion on its prey destruction is its way.
Forgiveness is the key to achieving harmony.
And one thing remains the same.
Best friends pulled apart. Distance causes broken hearts.
Two souls bound by love from the Father up above.
Like a dove a sign of peace in our hearts there will be.
This bond it will stay strong.
Through the sorrow and the pain I know one thing
Remains the same.

He is my rock. He is my salvation.
He is my defense. I will not be moved.

He alone is my rock and my salvation; he is my fortress, I will not be shaken.

Psalm 62:6

Reflections

_____

_____

_____

_____

_____

_____

_____

_____

_____

_____

_____

_____

_____

_____

_____

_____

_____

_____

_____

_____

_____

_____

_____

_____

_____

_____

_____

_____

_____

_____

_____

_____

_____

_____

The Voice

As I stare at the sunset I can't catch my breath.
The view is astonishing.
I watch till there's just a few pink streaks left.
My heart it is pounding. There's a tear in my eye.
Then I hear His still, small voice,
"Relax, child, it is I."
Sometimes in the midst of a very busy day
The burdens I carry start to get heavy.
The stress of the little things start to build up.
I close my eyes to push them away.
Then I hear His voice again,
"Relax, child, I'll show you the way."
It's raining again. There's despair in the air.
Each bolt of lightning gets closer and closer.
The thunder is fierce. I'm trembling with fear.
It's then that I hear,
"Relax, child, I'm right here."
My anxieties build up and become really hard to bear.
My mind is filled with thoughts that are so unreal and false.
The pressure is building up.
I wish the thoughts would stop.
Then I hear the voice,
"Relax, child, remember I'm your Rock."
Have you ever seen a rose in full bloom?
Its beauty is amazing. It's vibrant and alive.
The thorns on the stem remind me of the roads of life.
But it leads to something glorious; something sculpted with care.
Again I hear that still, small voice,
"Relax, child, you'll make it there."

Relax, child, I'm right here.

Do not be anxious about anything, but in everything, by prayer and petition, with thanksgiving, present your requests to God.

Philippians 4:6

Cast all your anxiety on him because he cares for you.

1 Peter 5:7

Reflections

_____
_____
_____
_____
_____
_____
_____
_____
_____
_____
_____
_____
_____
_____
_____
_____
_____
_____
_____
_____
_____
_____
_____
_____
_____
_____
_____
_____
_____
_____
_____
_____
_____
_____

Focus On Him

Here comes the rain. Here comes the pain.
Here come the tears. You know the fear.
This world is cruel, too many rules.
They don't agree with Him who sees.
All that we are. Sometimes we go too far.
When your focus is on Him, you will not go astray.
When your focus is on Him, He will show you the way.
Here comes payday. Here comes the bills.
Here comes the pain of financial strain.
No help for you. What should you do?
He says to tithe, but that leaves you dry.
So far in debt looks like there's no way out.
When your focus is on Him, you will not go astray.
When your focus is on Him, He will show you the way.
Focus on Him when things look grim.
Look to Christ when things aren't right.
Give Him your praise all of your days.
Hold on. Hold on. With Him, you can't go wrong.
When your focus is on Him, you will not go astray.
When your focus is on Him, He will show you the way.

Keep your focus on Him.
He will lead you on the right path.
When your focus is on Him, you will not go astray.
When your focus is on Him, He will show you the way.
When the world gets you down, and it's too much to bear-
When the world gets you down, remember Jesus is there.

Let us fix our eyes on Jesus, the author and perfecter of our faith, who for the joy set before him endured the cross, scorning its shame, and sat down at the right hand of the throne of God.

Hebrews 12:2

But I am afraid that just as Eve was deceived by the serpent's cunning, your mind may somehow be led astray from your sincere and pure devotion to Christ.

2 Corinthians 11:3

As he looked up, Jesus saw the rich putting their gifts into the temple treasury. He also saw a poor widow put in two very small copper coins. "I tell you the truth," he said, "this poor widow has put in more than all the others. All these people gave their gifts out of their wealth; but she out of her poverty put in all she had to live on."

Luke 21:1-4

Reflections

Remember Me

There are mornings when I wake up and rush to get ready for the day.
I run out of the house without a thought of you on my mind.
The traffic is slow. I hit every red light.
I'm standing in the longest lines no matter where I go.
The stress begins to build up. Then a thought occurs to me.
God's saying, "Did you remember me?"
As I walk though this life there are so many different roads to choose.
There are trials and tribulations. There are joys and celebrations.
Many times I feel as though I cannot take another step.
I have to try so very hard it seems to keep my focus all on you.
Day after day I say to you, "Can you help me one more time?"
Day after day you answer me, "You are a child of mine.
I am here to take your burdens. I am here to lend a helping hand.
Remember that I love you, and I am doing all I can."
So many good things have happened in my life:
Marriage, motherhood, and families richly blessed.
As always, I am grateful, but a concern that stays close to my heart
Is if it all ended tomorrow would I have lived my life in vain?
All that I can hope for is that you'll remember me.

I'm down on my knees, asking you please, when you return
Will you remember me? Cause I will be ready and waiting
To see you standing at my door.

Blessed is the man who perseveres under trial, because when he has stood
the test, he will receive the crown of life that God has promised to those
who love him.

James 1:12

Yet to all who received him, to those who believed in his name, he gave the
right to become children of God.

John 1:12

Reflections

Here I Am

The phone rings.
The baby cries.
One more hour in bed I'd like.
I look at the clock – 6:30 A.M.
It's time to face the world again.
So far from home
I'm feeling all alone.
My husband's still at work, and
I'm so tired I hurt.
I look at the clock – 7:30 P.M
I don't think this day is ever gonna end.
Can't fall asleep.
So much running through my mind.
Hear a little whimper.
Make sure the baby's alright.
I look at the clock – 2:30 A.M.
Where are you when I need ya?
Need some peace of mind.
My husband's off to work.
I'm left lying all alone.
A night of fitful sleep;
A new day the same song.
I look at the clock – 6:30 A.M.
I put my hands together and you say, "Here I am."

My spirit's broke down.
My mind is overwhelmed.
I can feel the pressure coming down all around.
The weight of the world is heavy on my shoulders.
And I stop…and look up and there you are with your arms open wide
And a smile you can't hide,
Saying, "Look…you did it again,
And all you need to know is here I am."

Then you will call, and the Lord will answer; you will cry for help, and he will say here I am.

Isaiah 58:9

Reflections

_____
_____
_____
_____
_____
_____
_____
_____
_____
_____
_____
_____
_____
_____
_____
_____
_____
_____
_____
_____
_____
_____
_____
_____
_____
_____
_____
_____
_____
_____
_____
_____
_____

He Created Me

O God you have created me. *You created my inmost being.*
All the days you have planned out for me
Were decided long before I was even meant to be.
You know the number of hairs on my head.
You chose the color of my eyes.
You decided just how tall I should be.
You have my birthday memorized.
You know each thought before I speak.
Each breath I take is planned.
You knew the choices I would make,
And that I would end up in this place.
You knew the day I would take your hand.
All the trouble I have faced is written down in a special place.
You know each tear that I have cried,
And the joy I felt when I came to your side.
I know you have blessings planned for me.
The road I travel I cannot foresee.
But I know that you'll take care of me
Just because you created me.
You know the day my life will end.
And when you come to take me home
I'll gladly come with you.
For it will be a joy to be
With the one who created me.

He created me.
He created me.
Everything that I see
Is because He created me.

For you created my inmost being; you knit me together in my mother's womb.

Psalm 139:13

Know that the Lord is God. It is he who made us, and we are his; we are his people, the sheep of his pasture.

Psalm 100:3

Reflections

Failure

Fail – to fall short, as in what is expected of one; to decline, as in strength or effectiveness.

Doesn't failure just prompt us to do it different next time all the while learning new things about ourselves? Never say never and never give up! We are a work in progress. God is not finished with us yet.

David also said to Solomon his son, "Be strong and courageous, and do the work. Do not be afraid or discouraged, for the LORD God, my God, is with you. He will not fail you or forsake you until all the work for the service of the temple of the LORD is finished."
1 Chronicles 28:20

For we do not have a high priest who is unable to sympathize with our weaknesses, but we have one who has been tempted in every way, just as we are – yet was without sin. Let us then approach the throne of grace with confidence, so that we may receive mercy and find grace to help us in our time of need.
Hebrews 4:15-16

Saved Again

I've said goodbye to my spouse, picked up the house, made the bed, fed the
dog and the kid.
I'm thinking this is great. I started at 8. I'm on a roll, and then I fall…
I haven't spent any time with him at all.
Temptation is always hard to bear. It seems to be floating in the air.
Do this. Do that temptation taunts. Easy living and quick rewards it flaunts.
It's so hard to just say no just because God says so. Even though I
give it my all
More often than not you'll see me fall.
Confess with your mouth that Christ is Lord.
Believe in your heart God rolled away the door.
With your heart believe and be justified. With your mouth confess
and be saved.
There is no difference between us all. The same Lord is Lord of all.
For everyone who calls, He will forgive your fall.
Do not judge. Do not condemn. In all your ways strive to be like him.
Give and give and then forgive. What an amazing way to live.
Love should be your main concern. That may be a hard lesson to learn.
Remember if you fall again, you can always call on him.
We all will sin and fall. Lord, please help us all.
No matter what we do, it's hard to keep our eyes on you.
Do not fear. Do not be afraid. Because of Him we all are saved.

I'm saved again and again and again. Every time I fall and get up and repent
I'm saved again and again and again. Again and again and again,
I'm saved again.

For the wages of sin is death, but the gift of God is eternal life in Christ
Jesus our Lord.

Romans 6:23

Reflections

Every Day

Sometimes I say things I didn't want to.
Sometimes I look at you in a way I didn't want to.
Sometimes I raise my voice when I didn't want to.
Thank goodness for my Lord because every day I fall short.
Sometimes I do things I didn't want to.
Sometimes I say yes when I should say no.
Sometimes I say no when I should say yes.
Thank goodness for my Lord because every day I fall short.
Sometimes my thoughts aren't that pure.
Sometimes my actions are undesirable.
Sometimes I forget who's really in control.
Thank goodness for my Lord because every day I fall short.
Sometimes I cause suffering and pain.
Sometimes I fight for my own personal gain.
Sometimes I walk down the wrong road.
Thank goodness for my Lord because every day I fall short.
Sometimes I serve myself and not my God.
Sometimes I love myself and not my God.
Sometimes I'm not the child that I should be.
Thank goodness for my Lord because every day I fall short.

Every day I fall short of the glory of God.
And every day I am freely justified by his grace
Through the redemption of his son.

For all have sinned and fall short of the glory of God, and are justified freely
by his grace through the redemption that came by Christ Jesus.
Romans 3:23-24

I do not understand what I do. For what I want to do I do not do,
but what I hate I do.
Romans 7:15

Reflections

Temptation

Temptation is the pull from our own evil thoughts.
I know you're thinking, "I'd never do that."
You must anticipate it. We don't grow out of it.
Let it be a warning to you.
He'll provide a way out, so you can stand up tall.
God is faithful, and he knows what you can handle.
The devil can only do what God allows him to do.
When you think you're standing firm, be careful you don't fall.
Admit temptation. You are not alone.
Ask God for help. Use his 24 hour phone.
Don't repress it, confess it.
Don't conceal it, reveal it.
The wise turn away. The foolish are careless.
The more we think about it, the more we want it.
The best solution is to just avoid it.
When you can't stand the temptation: Just focus on Him!
The devil made me do it: Is not an excuse!
The spirit is willing: But the body is weak!
All we need to do is: Keep choosing God!

Power, money, greed, lust
Worry, hunger, need, significance
Run, run, run
Temptations gonna get you
So, get ready, set, run.

When tempted, no one should say, "God is tempting me." For God cannot be tempted by evil, nor does he tempt anyone; but each one is tempted when, by his own evil desire, he is dragged away and enticed. Then, after desire has conceived, it gives birth to sin; and sin, when it is full-grown, gives birth to death.

James 1:13-15

"Watch and pray so that you will not fall into temptation. The spirit is willing, but the body is weak."

Matthew 26:41

No temptation has seized you except what is common to man. And God is faithful; he will not let you be tempted beyond what you can bear. But when you are tempted, he will also provide a way out so that you can stand up under it.

1 Corinthians 10:13

Reflections

Go His Way

O God, my Father in Heaven, how blessed I am today
To have your eyes always on me as I slowly go my way.
It's wonderful to see the way you've treated me.
I have the finer things in life, your love and mercy.

I'm on my way to be the person you see in me.
Gifts you've provided me are becoming clear to me.
As I strive to be the best for you and share the news for all to see,
Your hand will gently guide me on the path you have prepared for me.

Now I can very plainly see my only goal in life should be
To begin this very day, in everything, go his way.

If I go my way and forget to say
Be with me Lord all the way
I'll miss the point and start to stray.
But if I go his way every day
I'll be blessed in every way.

"I am the way and the truth and the life. No one comes to the Father except through me."

John 14:6

Submit yourselves, then, to God. Resist the devil, and he will flee from you. Come near to God and he will come near to you.

James 4:7-8

Reflections

_____
_____
_____
_____
_____
_____
_____
_____
_____
_____
_____
_____
_____
_____
_____
_____
_____
_____
_____
_____
_____
_____
_____
_____
_____
_____
_____
_____
_____
_____
_____

If I Choose Him

I could choose love or hate.
It's life versus death,
Joy or pain, full or hungry.
It's Him or me.
The choice is mine to make.

It's heaven or hell.
It's light versus dark,
Calm or stormy,
Living in day or night,
Doing good or evil.
The choice is mine to make.

I can be patient or impatient.
Be content or discontent.
It's dependence or independence.
I'll be faithful or unfaithful.
The choice is mine to make.

Hot heart or cold heart.
It's give versus take,
Forgive or hold a grudge,
His control or my control.
It's Him or me.
The choice is mine to make.

If I choose Him, then I choose love.
I choose to walk the path of truth.
When I choose Him, then I become
Full of His grace and love.

This day I call heaven and earth as witnesses against you that I have set before you life and death, blessings and curses. Now choose life, so that you and your children may live and that you may love the Lord your God, listen to his voice, and hold fast to him, for the Lord is your life.

Deuteronomy 30:19-20

"But if serving the Lord seems undesirable to you, then choose for yourselves this day who you will serve...But as for me and my household, we will serve the Lord."

Joshua 24:15

Reflections

Strength In Weakness

<u>Strength</u> – the power to resist attack; impregnability, the power to resist strain or stress; durability, the ability to maintain a moral or intellectual position firmly, capacity or potential for effective action.

There are just times when I can't do it. When I can admit that, it is so much easier to let God have it and take care of it his way. His way is always better. I can be so stubborn! When I turn it over, I am always amazed at how much more strength I actually have. I can do it, but only with his help.

But he said to me, "my grace is sufficient for you, for my power is made perfect in weakness." Therefore I will boast all the more gladly about my weaknesses, so that Christ's power may rest on me. That is why for Christ's sake, I delight in weaknesses, in insults, in hardships, in persecutions, in difficulties. For when I am weak, then I am strong.

2 Corinthians 12:9-10

Lord, Teach Me To Pray

Lord, teach me to pray
That I might find healing and be blessed
That I may see what others miss
And turn my sins in for forgiveness.
Lord, teach me to pray.
That I might seek and then find
That I might ask and then receive
And then knock and slip through that open door.
Lord, teach me to pray
That I might fall and then get up
That I might grieve and then release
And then bow down and praise your name.
Lord, teach me to pray
That I might find joy in suffering
That I might cry real tears of pain
And be honest to your face.
Lord, teach me to pray
That I might see footprints in the sand
And see you take me by the hand
And not alone will I stand.
Lord, teach me to pray
That I might have thankfulness
That I might feel your holiness
And walk through life a witness.

Teach me to pray, Lord.
Pour out my heart, Lord.
Open my eyes, Lord.
Teach me to pray.

One day Jesus was praying in a certain place. When he finished, one of his disciples said to him, "Lord, teach us to pray, just as John taught his disciples."

Luke 11:1

Reflections

_____
_____
_____
_____
_____
_____
_____
_____
_____
_____
_____
_____
_____
_____
_____
_____
_____
_____
_____
_____
_____
_____
_____
_____
_____
_____
_____
_____
_____
_____

Let Us Go

I need a place where I can go
To be myself,
To bare my soul.
A place where I
Can close my eyes
And feel the presence
Of my God.

I need a place where I can go
To learn the truth,
The word of God.
A place where I
Can be forgiven,
And know that I
Am headed for heaven.

I need a place where I can go
To fellowship
With Christian hearts.
A place where I
Can feel at home
To lift my voice
Up for my Lord.

I need a place where I can go
To feel the love
I cherish so.
A place where I
Can gather hope
To lead me through
This winding road.

I know a place where I can go
To share my gifts
With hopeless souls.
So I was glad
When someone said,
"Let us go
To the house of the Lord."

Let us go.
Let us go.
Let us go into the house of the Lord.
Let us go.
Let us go.
Let us go into the house of the Lord.

I rejoiced with those who said to me "Let us go to the house of the Lord."

Psalm 122:1

Reflections

Godly Woman

In society today, I must wear my hair a certain way.
I must maintain a certain weight, keep my body in great shape.
There's so much pressure to be someone we can't achieve.
I feel the appearance that should count comes from the inside out.

An example there must be. One I could follow closely,
One with outstanding abilities. A strong character has she.
Lord, do you have someone in mind? One that you could find?
An inspiration to be all I can be. O, Lord, can you help me?

He shows me a woman in Proverbs who has noble character.
I want to know more about her, this woman in Proverbs.
What makes her worth more than rubies? How does she have so much energy?
I see she is faithful and true. Noble is only one of her virtues.
She is strong and just keeps going. When does she have time to sleep?
She is reliable. It is undeniable.

She gives her all with open arms to those in need and her family.
She is wise and dignified, energetic and alive!
She watches over her house. She does not idle about.
Her children call her blessed. And what's this I almost missed?
Charm can be deceiving and outside beauty can be fleeting.
So, the most important parts do come from the inside out.

I want to be a strong, godly woman.
Help me be a strong, godly woman.
Give me wisdom, skills, and compassion and the fear of God in me,
To become a strong, godly woman.

Epilogue: The Wife of Noble Character

Proverbs 31:10-31

Charm is deceptive, and beauty is fleeting; but a woman who fears the Lord is to be praised. Give her the reward she has earned and let her works bring her praise at the city gate.

Proverbs 31: 30-31

Reflections

I Am The One

"I am the vine. You are the branches."
If you believe in me, I will be with you.
Without me, you will lose your way.
But stick with me and you will know peace.
If you love me, you will obey my command.
If you love me, we'll walk hand in hand.
Without me, you will lose your way.
Without me, Satan can take the lead.
Come out of the dark and walk into the light.
Light your candle. Let it burn so bright.
Let me know I am number one.
Hold on tight. Your life has just begun.
Repent your sins. You will be forgiven.
You'll have new life; a new identity.
You've earned the right to be a child of God.
Go tell the world what you believe.

I, I am the one through which all things can be done.
I, I am the one whose plan for you is good not harm.
I, I am the one. My kingdom will come. My will shall be done.
I, I am the one. Give me your life. With me you've won.

"For I know the plans I have for you", declares the Lord, "plans to prosper
you and not to harm you, plans to give you hope and a future."

Jeremiah 29:11

Repent, then, and turn to God, so that your sins may be wiped out,
that times of refreshing may come from the Lord.

Acts 3:19

"I am the vine; you are the branches. If a man remains in me and I in him,
he will bear much fruit; apart from me you can do nothing."

John 15:5

Reflections

I Will Be There

In the morning when you rise, when you see birds in the skies,
in a whisper, in the trees,
In a soft warm breeze I will be there.
I will be there.
As you're driving in your car, no matter where you are, in the sun, in the rain,
On a snowy, winter day I will be there.
I will be there.
In another person's smile, in another person's frown, when you're happy,
When you're sad, or if someone makes you mad I will be there.
I will be there.
Under a critic's sharp eye, in the middle of the night, times of pain,
times of trials,
Even through tomorrow I will be there.
I will be there.
When the sun is going down and there's quiet all around, in a prayer,
in a sigh,
When you close your eyes I will be there.
I will be there.
In every single day, in every single way, in the chaos, in the calm
I'll carefully guide you on. I will be there.
I will be there.

When you walk through the water, I will be there.
When you pass through the rivers,
I will be there. When you walk through the fire, I will be there, yes, I will.
I will be there. You know I will.

When you pass through the waters, I will be with you; and when you pass through the rivers, they will not sweep over you. When you walk through the fire, you will not be burned; the flames will not set you ablaze.

Isaiah 43:2

Reflections

Contentment Through Adversity

Content(ed) – desiring no more than what one has; satisfied, ready to accept or acquiesce; willing, satisfied with things as they are.

There is always a positive in all the negative, a light in the darkness, no matter how small and how hard you have to search for it. My favorite magnet I ever bought stated "Bloom where you are planted." In my mind, I knew I had written down a verse for contentment. I came across an old letter that my mom had sent me years ago as I was searching. The subject underlined was to gain contentment! I imagine she pulled it from a bible study she was doing at the time. Thank you God. And thank you mom!

1. Allow ourselves to complain of nothing, not even the weather. (Philippians 2:14)
2. Never picture ourselves in any circumstances in which we are not. (Philippians 4:11-13)
3. Never compare our lot with that of another. (2 Corinthians 10:12)
4. Never allow ourselves to wish that this or that had been otherwise. (Romans 8:28)
5. Never dwell on the morrow; remember that is God's and not ours. (Matthew 6:25-34)

And we know that in all things God works for the good of those who love him, who have been called according to his purpose.

Romans 8:28

This Race Called Life

We begin as a small individual-
A tiny little blessing from above.
As we grow we are slowly being molded
By the one who directs us how to run
In this race called life.
Along the way he will gently guide us.
He says make sure that your focus stays on him.
He promises to never leave you or forsake you.
So I may boldly say I will not fear
This race called life.
He won't promise that we won't run in to trouble.
He says that joy will come when we persevere.
If you call, then the Lord will surely answer.
When you cry for help he'll say, "I am here,"
In this race called life.
Trust in him, and he will guide you onward.
If you love him, you will obey what he commands.
Never cease to pray and love one another.
Heed his word, and you'll be blessed by the Son of man.
In this race called life.
He knows just what you need
And will give it up enthusiastically
When you make him first place
In this race.

This race, this race called life.
We will run this race called life.
God says just choose me and you'll make it home safely.
When we run this race called life.

Therefore, since we are surrounded by such a great cloud of witnesses, let us throw off everything that hinders and the sin that so easily entangles, and let us run with perseverance the race marked out for us.

Hebrews 12:1

Reflections

_____

_____

_____

_____

_____

_____

_____

_____

_____

_____

_____

_____

_____

_____

_____

_____

_____

_____

_____

_____

_____

_____

_____

_____

_____

_____

_____

_____

_____

_____

_____

_____

_____

_____

_____

_____

_____

_____

_____

Just Give Me Jesus

He's the creator of all things
And he's waiting in the wings.
Just give me Jesus. Just give me Jesus.
He sheds light on darkness.
He's a great investment.
Just give me Jesus. Just give me Jesus.
He's the best thing for your life.
And he's not a waste of time.
Just give me Jesus. Just give me Jesus.
If you're feeling emptiness,
Look to him for happiness.
Just give me Jesus. Just give me Jesus.
He's irresistible.
He's inescapable.
Just give me Jesus. Just give me Jesus.
Everything he sees.
He'll bring you to your knees.
Just give me Jesus. Just give me Jesus.
If you ask him from the start,
He will live within your heart.
Just give me Jesus. Just give me Jesus.
He can take away the pain.
You have everything to gain.
Just give me Jesus. Just give me Jesus.
For God so loved the world,
That he gave his only son.
If you believe in Him,
Eternally you've won.
Just give me Jesus. Just give me Jesus.

Just give me Jesus. He makes all things possible.
Just give me Jesus. He makes living wonderful.
Just give me Jesus. Just give me Jesus.

For God so loved the world that he gave his one and only Son, that whoever believes in him shall not perish but have eternal life.

John 3:16

Reflections

Dear Father

Dear Father,
Can you help me? I haven't talked with you since last night.
But as I sit here and wait for my baby boy to awake
I have a few joys and concerns on my mind.
Oh Father,
I want to thank you. I have a brand new day ahead.
The sun is shining, birds are singing, and the
Sweet sound of my son's breath can be heard.
I have a man in my life who is good to his wife.
Can you bring him home safely tonight?
My Father,
Can you bless me?
Can you enlarge my heart and mind for your good?
Can you keep your hand steady on me? Keep evil from me?
I don't want to cause any pain today.
Blessed Father,
How about some patience?
Mine can run so very thin.
Oh yes, and contentment?
My heart desires other places and things.
I need to focus on the one thing that I know to be true
And, oh Father, that's you.
Dear Father,
Thanks for listening.
I commit myself to you today.
I pray that you'll direct me on the paths I should follow.
I feel secure in knowing that you'll be watching over me
And giving me strength for the day.

Dear Father, can you help me?

You do not have because you do not ask God.

James 4:2

Good and upright is the Lord; therefore, he instructs sinners in his ways. He guides the humble in what is right and teaches them his way.

Psalm 25:8-9

Reflections

Knockin On My Door

I met the man of my dreams back in high school.
In college it just wasn't meant to be.
A few years later we were back together.
I don't know if it was fate or destiny.
Can ya hear that knockin on my door?
I'm 32 weeks along and I feel pressure.
2 months early, can he be?
It's a healthy baby boy.
I'm amazed as I can be.
Someone must be watchin over me.
Can ya hear that knockin on my door?
I love being at home with my new baby.
A stay-at-home mom I'd like to be.
2 months later a promotion to Decatur.
Is it a miracle or just a chance happening?
Can ya hear that knockin at my door?
A new home that's so far away from family.
New friends and new activities.
I'm so lonely that it hurts, and then I found a church.
Did the Holy Spirit just touch me?
I can finally hear that knockin on my door.
A move back to where I came from.
Divorce and a new identity.
Pain causes growth in me I didn't foresee.
Determination, strength, and dignity.
I can still hear ya knockin on my door.

I'm standin at the door just a knockin.
Won't ya please let me come in?
Oh, I'm standing at the door just a knockin.
Won't ya please let me come in?
I've given ya lots of chances, and still I'm here a standin.
Knock, knock, knockin at your door.

"Here I am! I stand at the door and knock. If anyone hears my voice and opens the door, I will come in and eat with him, and he with me.

Revelation 3:20

Reflections

180 Degrees

I don't pretend to know what's on your mind.
One day it's black. One day it's white.
I know there's one thing that is true.
You'll be with me through and through.
I know you think I've done a 180 turn.
My life has changed. I know it's true.
I can't wait for the day when you take my hand
And say, "My darling, I understand."
Some days it's hard for me to know
How far we've come and how far we'll go.
One step forward then two steps back.
I say too much. I don't say enough.
I get excited about small steps in this relationship.
I know there is a plan for you.
It will present itself in time.
I anxiously await the day
You exclaim to me, "I see the Light."
You work so hard. It's in your blood.
You provide for us. You stay so strong.
He gives you strength and cheers you on when I cannot.
He gave you character so bold,
A heart that loves and withstands the storms.
He may not get the credit now,
But I know in time it will come out.
The waiting is so very hard.
I get encouraged and then it all just seems to fall apart.
My character is not that strong.
Many times I want to throw in the towel.
I move on in faith and trust you see.
I know many times the changes needed
Are not in you they are in me.
But I know if I keep asking Him
I'll see you walk that 180 degrees.
I'm waiting for that happy day when I hear Him say,
"My son, I knew you'd turn this way."

I know you think I've done a 180 turn. My life has changed.
I know it's true. I can't wait for the day when you take my hand and say,
"My Darling, I understand."

It always protects, always trusts, always hopes, always perseveres.
Love never fails.

1 Corinthians 13:7-8

Reflections

_____
_____
_____
_____
_____
_____
_____
_____
_____
_____
_____
_____
_____
_____
_____
_____
_____
_____
_____
_____
_____
_____
_____
_____
_____
_____
_____
_____
_____
_____
_____
_____

Forever Love

Jesus loves you like I love you,
But Jesus loves you even more.

Like a garden needs the sunshine,
All God's children need Jesus' love.

As a candle lights the darkness,
So does Jesus light our lives.

He will be your friend and Savior,
If you let Him guide your life.

Jesus loves you like I love you
But Jesus loves you even more.

Whoever does not love does not know God, because God is love.

1 John 4:8

But God demonstrates his own love for us in this: while we were still sinners, Christ died for us.

Romans 5:8

Reflections

Joy – No Matter What

<u>Breathe</u> – to inhale and exhale air, to be alive; live, to pause
to rest or regain breath.

I always remember my mom saying, "This too shall pass." She still tells me
that. Things pass. Life goes on. One breath, one step at a time. We can do
this. Breathe. Just breathe.

Consider it pure joy, my brothers, whenever you face trials of many kinds,
because you know that the testing of your faith develops perseverance.
Perseverance must finish its work so that you may be mature and complete,
not lacking anything.

James 1:2-4

Let Your Light Shine

Turn your light on and hold it up high.
Find those in the dark and bring them into the light.
This is the season. There's always a reason
To let your light shine.

Let your light shine to brighten the road
For all those people who've lost their way.
This is the season. Jesus is the reason
To let your light shine.

Let your light shine so sinners, like you and me,
Can meet Jesus and truly believe.
This is the season. He is the reason
To let your light shine.

Let your light shine all over this world.
Let your light shine to every boy and girl.
This is the season. You've got a reason
To let your light shine.

This is the season. He is the reason
To let your light shine.

"You are the light of the world. A city on a hill cannot be hidden. Neither do people light a lamp and put it under a bowl. Instead they put it on its stand, and it gives light to everyone in the house. In the same way, let your light shine before men, that they may see your good deeds and praise your Father in heaven."

Matthew 5:14-16

Reflections

Give It All To Me

Every morning I go to meet him. I pull myself sleep-eyed from bed.
He waits for me in silence as I try to clear my head. The day was like no other.
It started out the same. And then he kindly looked at me and said,
"Do you believe?"
I believe that you can move mountains. I believe that you can calm the seas.
But can you help me to believe, Lord, that the mountain might be me?
Oh, I believe in God the Father. I believe in the Trinity.
I believe that the Father sent you to make a believer out of me.

Then He asked me, "Do you love me?" And I replied, "Lord, yes, I do."
I love that I can ask you anything. I love that you will answer truthfully.
And I love to see your blessings, playing out right in front of me.
Yes, I love all that you've created. I love the mountains, rocks, and trees.
I love the rising and the setting sun, reminding me that you truly are the one.

He asked, "But do you truly love me?" And again I said, "Yes, Lord, I do."
I love the way you tell your stories. I love your gentle, caring style.
I love the way you've carefully molded me into this child of God.
Dear Jesus, you know I love you. I love the guidance you provide.
I love it when you tell me that you're always by my side.

Then he requested, "Give it all to me." Give me your time,
your space, your energy.
Give me your joys, concerns, and burdens. Give up your life as you know it now.
Give your love and your forgiveness. Give your heart, your mind, and soul.
Give me all your desires and things. Give me your family. Give me priority.
Give it all to me.

He asked me, "Do you love me?" And I replied, "Lord, yes, I do."

Then he called the crowd to him along with his disciples and said: "If anyone would come after me, he must deny himself and take up his cross and follow me."

Mark 8:34

The third time he said to him, "Simon son of John, do you love me?" Peter was hurt because Jesus asked him the third time, "Do you love me?" He said, "Lord, you know all things; you know that I love you." Jesus said, "Feed my sheep."

John 21:17

Reflections

Singing His Praises

The birds and the trees and the plants and the bees-
The rocks and the springs and all things in between.
Singing His praises. Singing His praises.

The colors in the sky, the aromas in the air-
The seasons of the year, the entire planet earth.
Singing His praises. Singing His praises.

A newborn's smell and the joy that you feel
When the miracle of life is staring you in the eye,
Let us lift His name up high!

There is big and small and the short and the tall.
There's one creator and He made us all.
Singing His praises. Singing His praises.

Many don't believe there's no chance happenings.
There's no small coincidence. It always will be Him.
And to Him praises we will sing!

Sing! Sing His praises.
Sing! Sing His praises.
Our father is gracious.
So, sing! Sing His praises.

I will praise God's name in song and glorify him with thanksgiving.
Psalm 69:30

The earth is the Lord's, and everything in it, the world, and all who live in it.
Psalm 24:1

Sing praises to God, sing praises; sing praises to our King, sing praises. For God is the King of all the earth; sing to him a psalm of praise.
Psalm 47:6-7

Reflections

My Jesus

My Jesus sees me through the eyes of his Father.
He watches over me night and day.
He protects me with his love, shields me from the storms,
My Jesus.
I'm encouraged by the whisper of his voice in the wind.
He tells me to be confident in all things.
He says hold your head up high. Look people in the eye.
My Jesus.
My Jesus knows when my heart is heavy with burdens.
He says release them to my Father up above.
He looks me square in the eyes.
He says, "You know I'm by your side."
My Jesus.
Father, thank you for your only son.
I'm more grateful for him every day.
I can smile from deep inside.
I have a better grasp on life with
My Jesus.

My Jesus, son to the Lord up above.
His protector chosen just for me.
My Jesus.

Be still, and know that I am God;

Psalm 46:10

"Come to me, all you who are weary and burdened, and I will give you rest.
Take my yoke upon you and learn from me, for I am gentle and humble
in heart, and you will find rest for your souls. For my yoke is easy and my
burden is light."

Matthew 11:28-30

Reflections

I Want To Thank You

I feel joy. I feel love.
I've been blessed from above.
Every day of my life
You'll be right by my side.
If there's pain in my heart,
I'll look to you from the start.
If I pray for relief,
You'll help me through the grief.
In the dark of the night,
When I think of scary things,
Close my eyes He is there.
He gives me a song to sing.
Train a child in your ways
He'll follow you all his days.
This is my hope for my sons.
I know with you they've won.
In the Bible is your truth.
You are the way the truth and light.
I'm so glad I've found you.
You've given me a brand new life.

I want to thank you
For giving me new life.
I want to thank you
For being by my side.
I want to thank you.
Thank you.
Thank you.

Give thanks to the Lord, for he is good.

Psalm 136:1

But thanks be to God. He gives us the victory through our Lord Jesus Christ.

1 Corinthians 15:57

Reflections

Calling Your Name

The mountains cry out, Jesus.
The birds sing out, Jesus.
The oceans call out, Jesus.
Feel them calling your name.

The poor want you, Jesus.
The rich want you, Jesus.
The weak and strong want you, Jesus.
They're calling your name.

The children love you, Jesus.
Every race loves you, Jesus.
I love you, Jesus.
We're calling your name.

Every heart needs you, Jesus.
Every soul needs you, Jesus.
We all need you, Jesus.
Come bring us home.

Jesus!
Whoa, whoa, whoa Jesus!
Yeah, yeah, yeah, Jesus!
I need you, Jesus!
I'm calling your name!

Find rest, O my soul, in God alone; my hope comes from him.

Psalm 62:5

Rich and poor have this in common; the Lord is the Maker of them all.

Proverbs 22:2

Above all else, guard your heart, for it is the wellspring of life.

Proverbs 4:23

Jesus said, "Let the little children come to me, and do not hinder them, for the kingdom of heaven belongs to such as these."

Matthew 19:14

Reflections

GOD IS GOOD
ALL THE TIME—
ALL THE TIME
GOD IS GOOD

Connect with the author and learn more about *My Heart's Therapy*

Twitter: @aheartstherapy

CPSIA information can be obtained
at www.ICGtesting.com
Printed in the USA
FSOW03n2331290316
18596FS